The Invaders

Written by Theodore Rowland-Entwistle
Illustrated by David Marshall

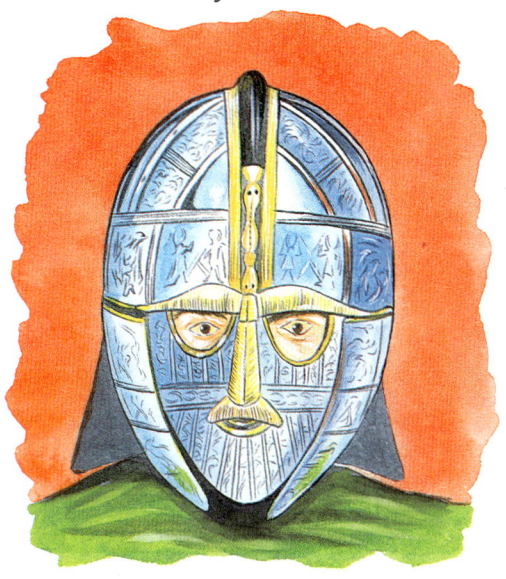

© 1994 Henderson Publishing Limited

THE INVADERS

British history is a story of repeated invasions. Some were peaceful, others involved great battles.

The first invaders were Stone Age people. They made all their tools of stone, using sharp flakes of flint as knives, scrapers and arrowheads.

They were followed by the Ancient Britons, the Celts and the Romans.

Britain Under Ice
Throughout the life of planet Earth, science tells us, great sheets of ice have spread from the North and South Poles. Each of these Ice Ages lasted for thousands of years. Between the last three Ice Ages, the earliest people settled in Britain. They left very few traces.

The last Ice Age began about 115,000 years ago, and ended as recently as 12,000 years ago. The ice did not cover the whole of Britain. It stopped roughly at a line from the Thames to the Severn estuary.

By Land to Europe
During the Ice Ages, a lot of water was locked up in the ice. As a result the sea level was much lower than it is today.

Britain was linked to the rest of Europe by dry land. The sea finally broke through at the Straits of Dover about 8,000 years ago. Until then animals and people could migrate into Britain overland.

Early Plant Life
Many of our familiar trees flourished in the south of Britain, clear of the ice cap. They included hazel, oak, pine, alder and elm. Ash and beech probably arrived later.

STONEHENGE

On the bare, wind-swept Salisbury Plain is the great monument of Stonehenge. It was built by people whose ancestors migrated into England from Brittany in France.

Stonehenge is a series of stone circles. The earliest circles were begun nearly 5,000 years ago.

That was 200 years before the Ancient Egyptians built the Great Pyramid. Stonehenge was completed about 3,500 years ago. These ancient builders were hard workers. The biggest stones weigh about 50 tonnes each. They were dragged on sledges more than 30 kilometres across the plain.

A smaller group of blue stones were brought, by water and overland, more than 200 kilometres from the Preseli Mountains in Wales. The stones are arranged so that the rising Sun on midsummer day shone between the upright stones on an altar. Stonehenge was probably used for astronomical observations and religious ceremonies.

GRIMES GRAVES

Stone Age Britons dug mines in the chalk to find flint for making their knives, axes, arrowheads and scrapers. They had open-air 'factories' where the flints were worked. Great heaps of partly-shaped flints and flint fragments have been found.

The largest mine is Grime's Graves, near Thetford in Norfolk. It is the biggest in Europe. Its 350 shafts go nearly 12 metres deep into the chalk. Horizontal passages lead from the bottom of the shafts. Grime's Graves supplied flint, possibly roughly shaped, to most of southern England.

Silbury Hill

One of the biggest mysteries of Stone Age Britain is Silbury Hill, which stands beside the A4 road in Wiltshire. It is the largest man-made mound in Europe, and it must have taken at least ten years to build. But nobody knows why it was built. Big earth mounds were usually made to hide tombs, but there is no grave under Silbury Hill. The hill is too small to be a fort. Possibly it was a look-out point.

THE INVADERS

SKARA BRAE

Skara Brae is an ancient village in mainland Orkney. It was inhabited for about 600 years, but was buried by sand during a storm 4,500 years ago. The village was rediscovered in the 1860s and gives a good picture of what life was like in the Stone Age. The people lived in stone huts, whose walls were plastered with clay on the outside. The roofs were probably made of wood, covered with skins or turf.

Each hut had a drain which led into a main sewer. There was a fire in the centre of the hut, and near it stone shelves like a modern dresser. There were bed places beside the fire. The people ate meat and fish, but grew no cereals. They apparently wore animal skins and bead necklaces. They made pottery, and played games with bone dice.

THE INVADERS

PREHISTORIC SCOTLAND

- The landscape was very different then. The hills were covered with forests and scrub, which was cleared in prehistoric times for timber and fuel.

- The valleys were largely marshland. The coast line moved outward as the land rose after the end of the Ice Age. For example, a cave near Oban where early people made their home used to lie on the seashore. It is now inland and some way above sea level.

The Picts

One tribe was called Picts, meaning 'painted people', by the Romans. The Picts apparently tattooed themselves. They were partly Celtic, but spoke a language which contained remains of a much older tongue. The Picts repeatedly raided the Roman settlements in northern Britain.

HILL FORTS

The Ancient Britons constructed many hill forts, especially in southern England. They built ramparts around the tops of suitable flat-topped hills.

In the early days much of the countryside around the hills was either marshland or forest. So hilltops were good places to live.

One important hill fort is Maiden Castle, in Dorset. It was built during the Iron Age, about 300 years before the Romans invaded Britain.

Hill forts were fortified towns, with many huts and other timber buildings inside the ramparts.

ISLANDS OF TIN

- After the Stone Age came the Bronze Age, when people started using bronze (an alloy of copper and tin) to make tools and weapons. In Britain the Bronze Age began about 3,800 years ago.
- Bronze was introduced by a group of people known as the Beaker Folk, because they made beakers as drinking vessels. Like all the invaders, they came from mainland Europe.
- With bronze, people could make better knives and other tools. They also made bronze food vessels. The ancient Greeks and Romans called Britain and its offshore islands the Islands of Tin. British miners dug tin in Cornwall. It was shipped to the Mediterranean countries, and was Britain's first important export.

THE INVADERS

IRON AGE

Iron came into Britain around 2,500 years ago. Bronze is not so much used now, but we are still in the Iron Age! England has large deposits of iron ore. It was worked in the Weald of Kent and Sussex for hundreds of years. Most of the forests of that area were cut down to heat the furnaces that smelted the iron.

If you come across names like Furnace Lane or Gun Hill you can be sure you are near ancient iron workings, which were in use up until the AD 1700s.

THE CELTS

The people who brought the use of iron into Britain were the Celts. They came originally from central Europe, where they were among the first people to use iron.

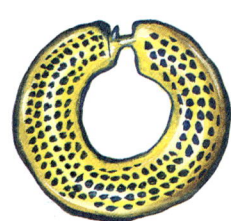 

The present day descendants of the Celts speak a group of languages known as Celtic. These languages include Welsh, Scottish and Irish Gaelic, and the almost forgotten language, Cornish. Across the English Channel, the Bretons of Brittany also speak a Celtic language, not unlike Cornish.

The Celts invaded Britain about 2,500 years ago. By the time the Romans arrived, 500 years later, Celtic tongues had replaced the original British languages.

Celtic Art

The Celts were skilled workers in metal, pottery and sculpture. Their art developed in western Europe. Celtic art died out in continental Europe before the Roman invasion of Britain, but it flourished in Britain for hundreds of years.

The Belgae

When the Romans first landed, the Britons they encountered were descendants of an advanced Celtic tribe, the Belgae. They settled in Kent and Essex.

The Belgae brought the use of the plough into Britain, and began an agricultural revolution. They built towns, and organised a number of small kingdoms in south-eastern England. Many of these kingdoms were united under the overlordship of Cymbeline. When he died, he divided his kingdom between his two sons, Caratacus and Togodumnus. This made Britain weak, and gave the Romans an opportunity to take over.

NORTHERN STRONGHOLDS

Celtic settlers in Scotland were warlike. Many of their strongholds survive. The earliest fortified houses in southern and eastern Scotland were built of timber, but later the Celtic Scots used stone.

In the north and west there was little timber available, and all defences were of stone, without mortar. A typical fortification was the broch, a stone tower with walls nearly five metres thick. The height varied between seven and thirteen metres.

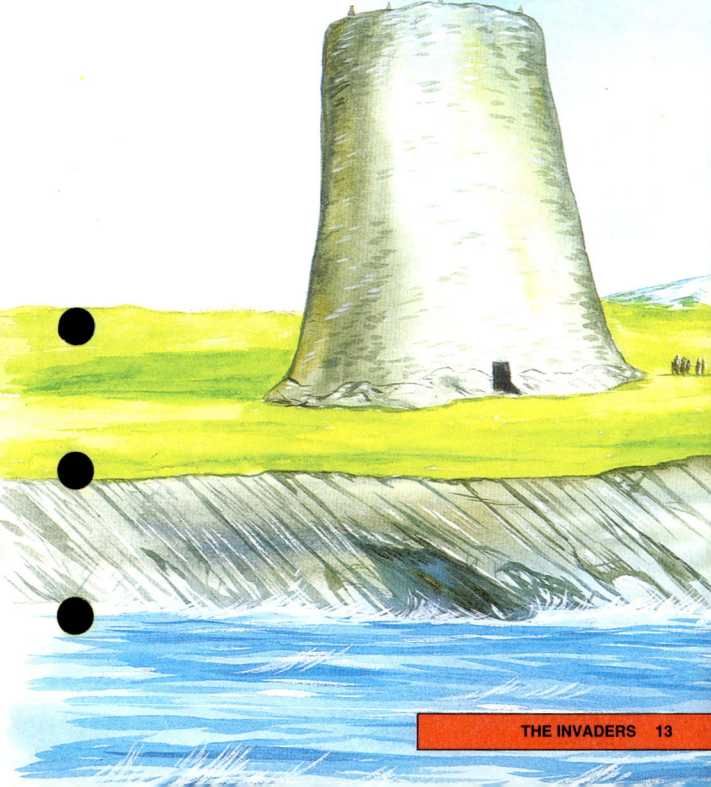

ENTER CAESAR

The first Roman to invade Britain was Julius Caesar, the Roman governor of Gaul (France). He landed at Deal in Kent in 55 B.C. He was probably trying to find Gaulish rebels who had retreated to Britain.

The Britons resisted fiercely, and when early winter storms damaged his ships Caesar decided to withdraw. He returned the next year with a stronger army, and forced the Britons in Kent to submit. Again he had to withdraw to avoid the winter storms.

BRITONS CONQUERED

Claudius's Expedition
After the departure of Caesar the Britons traded with the Romans. They exchanged grain and other raw materials for luxury goods.

Nearly one hundred years later, the Roman emperor Claudius sent an army of nearly 50,000 soldiers to conquer Britain. Many Romans regarded Claudius as a fool. He needed a military victory to improve his reputation. So he too arrived in Britain, about two months after the first landings.

He was in time to see the capture of Colchester, the British capital, and to accept the formal surrender of the Britons.

The Roman Advance
Within a few years the Romans had established a fortified line running from Devon to Lincolnshire.

Caratacus, the last British king of southern England, fled to Wales. From there he launched attacks on the Roman lines. The Romans captured him in 51 A.D., and went on to seize Anglesey, headquarters of the Druids.

THE DRUIDS

The Druids were the priests of the Celts who occupied Britain. They worshipped many gods, and revered oak and mistletoe. They were reputed to indulge in human sacrifice.

When the Roman soldiers met the British army in Anglesey, they saw Druids uttering prayers to their gods and curses on the enemy.

Women in black with flaming torches roamed throughout the line of battle, encouraging their men. The Romans were at first too terrified to attack. Then they recovered, and overthrew the Britons and the Druids.

BRAVE BOUDICCA

After only **17** years of Roman rule, a major revolt was led by Boudicca, Queen of the Iceni tribe in Norfolk. She rebelled because Roman soldiers had ill-treated her and her two daughters.

Boudicca gathered a large army, with the help of neighbouring tribes. She faced little opposition, because a large part of the Roman army was away in Wales, subduing Anglesey. The angry Britons sacked and destroyed Colchester, London and Verulamium (St Albans). They took no prisoners, and butchered thousands of Romans and their allies.

Eventually the Roman troops returned from Wales and met Boudicca's army somewhere in the Midlands. The Britons were heavily defeated. Boudicca escaped, but killed herself soon afterwards.

HADRIAN'S WALL

When the conquering British legions reached Scotland they found a bleak land, inhabited by fierce Picts.

The Emperor Hadrian, visiting Britain in 122, A.D. decided to build a wall across northern England to mark the frontier of the Roman province of Britain.
Hadrian's Wall runs from the Solway Firth to the River Tyne. It consisted of a stone wall with a ditch on the north side. Much of it still remains.

ROMAN ROADS

- The Roman army built magnificent roads all over the British province, so that they could move troops and supplies easily.
  Many modern roads still follow those routes. For example, the A1 Great North Road from London is the old Roman Ermine Street as far as York, and then follows the Roman Dere Street into Northumberland.

- The Romans built their roads on a solid basis of rubble, capped with flat stones. The road had a raised crown, or centre, so that water drained off, and ditches either side to carry the water away. Main roads were as much as three metres wide.

THE SCOTS ARRIVE

The Scotti were a group of people who migrated from Ireland to settle in Argyllshire, in south-western Scotland. They eventually gave their name to the whole country.

They formed a kingdom called Dalriada. Their language eventually became what we now call Scottish Gaelic. Their invasion began probably in the AD 300s.

A little later, Angles from the south formed the kingdom of Northumbria, which extended from England into what is now southern Scotland.

20 THE INVADERS

END OF ROMAN RULE

- In the late 300s the Romans began withdrawing troops from Britain to defend other parts of the empire against attacks by barbarian tribes.
- The last legion left in 406. The departing Romans buried their treasure 'so that no man might find it'.
- For hundreds of years nobody did, but in recent years several treasure hoards have been discovered, partly with the aid of metal detectors.

The Britons remaining largely followed Roman customs and laws, but they did not have the military power and skill to fight off barbarian attacks.

A NEW AGE BEGINS

The Middle Ages
Historians divide history into three main periods. Ancient history covers the earliest known written records to the fall of the Roman Empire.

The Middle Ages run from the fall of the Roman Empire to the capture of Constantinople by the Turks in 1453. All history since 1453 is known as the modern period. These divisions of time are purely for convenience. When the Middle Ages began nobody said 'Gosh, gee, it's the Middle Ages now'!

Appeal for Help
After the last Roman legions left, the Britons were under constant attack from the Angles, Saxons and Jutes, as well as from the Picts.

In despair, the Britons sent a desperate appeal for help to Rome, saying: 'The barbarians drive us into the sea, and the sea drives us back to the barbarians!' But the short answer from the Emperor Honorius was that they must look to their own defence.

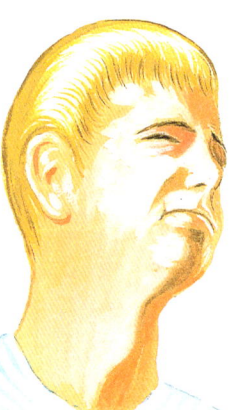

A FOLK HERO

King Arthur
King Arthur of the story books is a fictitious character. Most of the romantic legends about him were made up in the Middle Ages. But many scholars think there was a real Arthur. The Roman form of his name was Artorius. He was probably a British High King, and a war leader who did what Honorius suggested, and carried on the fight against the invaders.

The Real Arthur?
Some scholars believe Arthur is identical with an historical warrior known as Riothamus, who lived in the 400s.

Riothamus, like the Arthur of romance, led an expedition to Gaul to attack the Saxons. He was last heard of in 470. Riothamus is a Latin version of a British title, meaning something like 'High King'. So Riothamus's given name could well have been Arthur.

TREACHERY

Hengest and Horsa

Picts from the north raided England as far south as Kent. A British king known as Vortigern - which may be a title rather than a name - invited mercenary troops from Europe to help drive the Picts out.

The mercenaries were Angles from southern Denmark, led by two brothers, Hengest and Horsa. They landed at Ebbsfleet, near Ramsgate, Kent, in 449.

After driving away the Picts, Hengest and Horsa then turned on Vortigern and his people at Aylesford, near Maidstone, Kent. Horsa was killed in the battle. Hengest and his son Aesc went on to conquer Kent. In 488 Aesc became king of Kent and reigned for 34 years.

EARLY CONVERTS

Christianity
The Christian religion was introduced into Britain some time in the early AD 200s. For many years the British Christian Church was scattered and struggling.

In 325, when the Emperor Constantine decreed that Christianity should be the official religion of the Roman Empire, the British Church was sufficiently flourishing to have three bishops, at London, York and Lincoln.

When the Saxons overran Britain they brought their own religion with them. They worshipped Norse gods such as Woden and Thor, whose names are remembered in the days of the week.

During the Saxon invasions the Church went underground. Celtic missionaries from Ireland did their best to convert the Saxons.

Angelic Slaves

In 585 Abbot Gregory saw some fair-haired British boys for sale in the slave market in Rome. He asked who they were and was told 'Angles'.

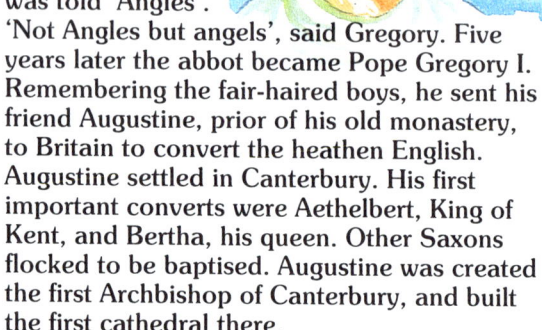

'Not Angles but angels', said Gregory. Five years later the abbot became Pope Gregory I. Remembering the fair-haired boys, he sent his friend Augustine, prior of his old monastery, to Britain to convert the heathen English. Augustine settled in Canterbury. His first important converts were Aethelbert, King of Kent, and Bertha, his queen. Other Saxons flocked to be baptised. Augustine was created the first Archbishop of Canterbury, and built the first cathedral there.

The Monasteries

Monasteries played an important part in British life. Monks were among the few people who could read and write.

OUR HERITAGE

Beowulf is a long poem in Old English, the language spoken by the Anglo-Saxons. It was probably written down somewhere around AD 700. It was the first major work in English. The poem tells of the heroic deeds of the warrior Beowulf in Sweden. In his youth he fights and kills a monster named Grendel.

In old age he fights a dragon, but both he and the dragon are mortally wounded. Although most of the Beowulf story is fiction, the background and other people mentioned in the poem were real.

SUTTON HOO

An exciting find at Sutton Hoo, in Suffolk, revealed armour, drinking vessels, money, a musical instrument and weapons of the AD 600s. There were also 41 gold objects and many silver objects.

The find was concealed under a barrow (an earth mound), and was a memorial to an East Anglian king, possibly King Raedwald, who died in 630.

The finds were in the remains of a ship 27 metres long. It was a Norse tradition to bury a warrior in his ship, but there was no skeleton at Sutton Hoo. The king may have died at sea or in another country.

A CATHOLIC COUNTRY

Theodore of Tarsus
In 667 Wighard, a Saxon priest, went to Rome to be consecrated as Archbishop of Canterbury. But he died before the ceremony could be performed.

Instead Pope Vitalian consecrated an elderly Greek monk, Theodore of Tarsus, as archbishop. Theodore was not even a priest at the time, so the choice was a surprise. Theodore turned out to be a very good archbishop. He quickly set about reorganising the Church in England, which badly needed it. Much of the organisation he set up still exists.

Adrian of Canterbury
Theodore was not Pope Vitalian's first choice. That was Adrian, abbot of a monastery near Monte Cassino in Italy. Adrian refused the post, but agreed to go with Theodore to help him.

His great achievement was in developing the school at the monastery of St Augustine, Canterbury. As a result, England gained many scholars who spoke fluent Greek and Latin, and knew astronomy and mathematics.

PIRATES

The Force
To people today, 'The Force' usually means the police force. To Anglo-Saxon monks, writing the history of their times, it meant the Vikings.
Viking was a Norse word that meant 'pirate'. These pirates came from Scandinavia. They are also known as Norsemen, people from the north, or as Danes. The Anglo-Saxons were pirates themselves when they first attacked and settled in Britain.

In 787 they themselves faced attacks by pirates when the Vikings began raiding England.

THE INVADERS

A Viking Raid

At home the Vikings were mostly peaceful farmers, some were fierce warriors and bold sailors. When good farmland became scarce in Scandinavia, they set out to find new lands. A Viking raid was a bloodthirsty attack. The Norsemen looted and burned villages and towns. They killed any men who opposed them, and carried off the most beautiful women. The first raids were just for looting. Later some Vikings began to settle, especially in northern England.

The Danelaw

The part of Britain occupied by the Vikings or Danes became known as the Danelaw. It varied in size from time to time.

You can still see which parts of the country were under Danish or Viking rule by the place names. For example, names ending in -by, meaning a dwelling-place, are Scandinavian. Examples are Derby and Whitby. Another Scandinavian name is Thwaite, as in Norfolk.

FIRST KINGS

The English Kingdoms
England under the Anglo-Saxons was divided into a number of small kingdoms. They included Wessex, the kingdom of the West Saxons, Sussex (South Saxons) and Essex (East Saxons). Others were Northumbria, Mercia and Kent.

Wessex was one of the most powerful, and it led the resistance to the Danish invaders.

Egbert
Egbert, king of Wessex from 802 to 839, was the first man who could claim to be king of all England.

The kings of Mercia and Northumbria acknowledged him as their Bretwalda, meaning Lord of Britain.

DOWN WITH THE DANES

Offa's Dyke
Offa's Dyke is a huge earth rampart and ditch which runs from the River Severn to the River Dee. It was built by Offa, king of Mercia from 757 to 796 to keep out the Welsh, who had invaded Mercia. Parts of the dyke are still in good condition.

During Offa's reign Mercia was the most powerful kingdom in England.

Alfred the Great
Egbert's grandson, Alfred the Great, was the finest of the Saxon kings. His three brothers, Aethelbald, Aethelbert and Aethelred I, were kings before him. Aethelred and his surviving brother, Alfred, fought many battles against the Danes. When Aethelred died in 871, Alfred became king.

Alfred did not enjoy good health, but he fought doggedly on. Eventually he defeated the Danes, and divided England with them.

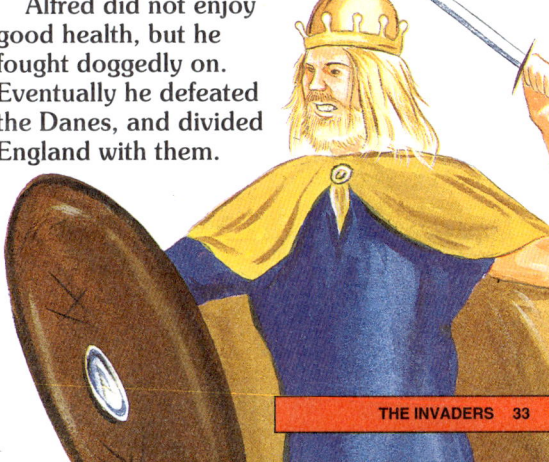

Alfred and the Cakes

After one defeat Alfred had to retreat to Athelney, in Somerset. It was then an island where two rivers met.

Tradition tells how he took shelter in a cottage. The housewife allowed him to sit by the fire provided he kept an eye on the cakes she was cooking there. Alfred was so busy thinking what to do next that he let the cakes burn. The housewife, not knowing who he was, scolded him severely.

Statesman and Scholar

Alfred was a wise statesman. He reorganised the government of his lands, and built a fleet.

He was also a scholar. He set out to revive learning, which had almost perished because the Danes had destroyed so many monasteries. Alfred founded new monasteries. He had Latin books translated into English, and probably did some of the translation himself.

FOR THE RECORD

The Anglo-Saxon Chronicle
During Alfred's reign a group of monks began to compile a history of England, known today as the Anglo-Saxon Chronicle.

The Chronicle continued up to the end of the reign of Stephen in 1154. It is a valuable source of information about the events of the period. It was written in English, rather than the Latin which was the main language of the Church.

Reconquering the Danelaw

Wessex under Alfred included all of England south-west of a line from London to Chester. The Danelaw extended north from there to a line running from the River Tees in the east to the Lake District.

Alfred's son, Edward the Elder, came to the throne in 899. He set out to reconquer the Danelaw. He was helped by his sister, Aethelflaed, who was the widow of King Aethelred of Mercia. At the end of Edward's 25-year reign brother and sister had conquered all of the Danelaw south of the Humber.

INTO BATTLE

The Battle of Brunanburh

Athelstan, Edward's elder son, continued the conquest of the northern lands. He began with Northumbria, an eastern kingdom which extended from the Tees to the Forth. Then he attacked the Scots of Strathclyde, the kingdom which lay to the west of Northumbria.

Three years later Olaf, leader of the Viking Danes in Ireland, invaded Britain and formed an alliance with the kings of Strathclyde and Alba (an old name for Scotland north of Hadrian's Wall). Athelstan and his brother Edmund defeated them at the Battle of Brunanburh. Five kings, plus seven earls from Ireland, died in the fight.

Nobody knows exactly where the battle was fought.

TURBULENT SCOTS

Kenneth MacAlpine
The beginning of Scotland as a kingdom was due to Kenneth MacAlpine, king of the Scots of Dalriada. He became king of the Picts as well. We do not know how he managed that. Many Picts objected, but Kenneth crushed them and by 850 was king over the united kingdom of Alba.

Thirteen kings followed Kenneth. We know little about the first nine, but the next four all died violent deaths.

Malcolm II
The first king of Scotland as we know it today was Malcolm II, who became king in 1005. He ruled not only Alba but also the British kingdom of Strathclyde. Orkney, Shetland and the Western Isles were ruled by the Norse kings of Scandinavia.

Malcolm left the kingdom to his grandson, Duncan I, who was the son of Malcolm's daughter Bethoc. Malcolm was a strong king, but Duncan was weak.

PEACEFUL TIME

St Dunstan

The next important king of Wessex was Edgar, known as 'the Peaceable'. He was influenced by Dunstan, Archbishop of Canterbury, who was his chief adviser.

Edgar's 16-year reign was quiet. This gave Dunstan a chance to carry on Alfred the Great's work of encouraging learning. Dunstan improved discipline in the monasteries. He was a skilled musician, metalworker and scribe. People revered him as a saint.

Kings at the Oars

In 973 Edgar visited Chester, where six other British kings came to him. They swore fealty (loyalty) to Edgar. According to tradition the kings then rowed him along the River Dee from Chester to the church of St John and back. Edgar steered the boat.

KINGS OF ENGLAND

Edward the Martyr
King Edgar died suddenly in 975, leaving two sons, neither of them really old enough to rule the kingdom. The elder son, Edward, was crowned king, but he had sudden bursts of rage which made him unpopular.

Edgar was on good terms with his stepmother, Aelfrida, and his half-brother Aethelred. But while he was on a visit to them he was murdered. Many people believed Aelfrida ordered the killing. People looked at the new king, Aethelred II, with suspicion. Meanwhile Edward was revered as a martyr and a saint.

The Evil-Counselled King
Aethelred was a weak king, always unsure of himself. He was also badly advised by his counsellors. He became known as 'Aethelred the Unraed', which means 'Evil-Counselled'. The Saxon word 'unraed' was later translated as 'unready', which was also a good description of this unhappy king.

Aethelred was married twice, the first time to a Saxon woman. Later he married Emma, sister of Duke Richard of Normandy.

THE INVADERS

Danegeld

Viking raids on England were renewed in Aethelred's reign. They were led by two kings, Olaf of Norway and Swein of Denmark.

The raiders defeated the Saxons in several battles, and Aethelred was forced to make terms. He bought peace in 991 by paying them a large sum of money as ransom.

Aethelred raised the money by a tax, which became known as Danegeld, or 'Dane gold'. The Danes were not satisfied with just one bribe. They carried on raiding, and were bought off by more payments of Danegeld.

THE FIGHT GOES ON

- **The Massacre of St Brice**
  In 1002 Aethelred was alarmed by a rumour that the Danes planned to murder him and his counsellors. So he ordered that all Danes in England should be killed on St Brice's Day, November 13.

Many Danes were massacred on that day, among them Gunnhild, the sister of Swein of Denmark. In revenge the Danes raided England several times in the next few years, collecting more Danegeld. Finally a major invasion left Swein as master of the country. In 1013 Aethelred fled to Normandy, which was when he married Emma. Swein was proclaimed king of England.

THE INVADERS 41

Edmund Ironside

Swein was not king of England for long. He died in 1014, and the English called Aethelred back. Danish attacks were resumed, led by Swein's son Cnut (often called Canute).

Aethelred died in 1016. Edmund, his son by his first wife, carried on the fight. His courage in battle earned him the nickname of 'Ironside'.

Edmund and Cnut agreed to divide the country. Edmund ruled south of the Thames, and Cnut ruled to the north. But Edmund died suddenly a few weeks later at the age of about 23, and Cnut became king of all England.

Cnut and the Waves

Cnut ruled England well. He was a Christian, and supported the Church. He tried to make his position safer by marrying Emma of Normandy, the widow of Aethelred II.

In 1018 Cnut succeeded his brother Harald as king of Denmark, and he later added Norway to his empire. His courtiers flattered him by saying he was all-powerful. Cnut had a chair placed on the seashore when the tide was coming in. He sat in it and ordered the waves to retreat. When the waves wetted his feet Cnut turned to the courtiers and said: 'You see? Only God is all-powerful.'

WEAK AND STRONG

Macbeth
Back in Scotland there was a rival claimant to the throne of Alba: Macbeth, the provincial ruler of Moray. Macbeth was probably Malcolm II's nephew, and his claim to the throne was as good as that of Duncan I.

In 1040, only six years after he became king, Duncan was killed in battle with Macbeth. It seems likely that Duncan was trying to get rid of Macbeth. Macbeth was a strong ruler. He occupied the throne for 17 years and was generous to the Church.

Edward the Confessor
In 1042, Edward, son of Aethelred II, was proclaimed king. Edward was a very pious man, known as 'Edward the Confessor'. Edward lived like a monk, so his wife had no children. Godwin, and from 1053, his son Harold Godwinsson, ruled the country in Edward's name.

THE INVADERS 43

Malcolm Canmore

Meanwhile in Scotland the rivalry for the throne went on. In **1057** Duncan I's son Malcolm III attacked and killed King Macbeth in battle at Lumphanan, in Mar.

The following year Malcolm killed Macbeth's stepson, Lulach, and made himself king of all Alba. Malcolm III was known as Canmore, which means 'big head'.

He spent several years as a boy at the court of Edward the Confessor of England, where he was safe from Macbeth.

Harold's Oath

Who was going to succeed Edward the Confessor as King of England? William, Duke of Normandy, claimed that Edward had promised to make him the heir. But Harold Godwinsson was already the ruler of England in all but name.

In 1064 Harold was shipwrecked on the coast of France, and fell into William's hands. William tricked Harold into swearing a solemn oath that he would help the duke to the English throne.

44 THE INVADERS

Harold II

When Edward the Confessor was dying he named Harold Godwinsson as the heir. The Saxon council, the Witan, agreed.

In January 1066 Earl Harold was proclaimed king as Harold II. He believed that the oath he had sworn to William was not binding, because William had made him take it by force. But many pious people thought the oath was binding, and they feared for Harold.

Halley's Comet

Soon after Harold became king Halley's Comet appeared in the sky. This comet returns to pass round the Sun about every 76 years. The Anglo-Saxons of England were startled by this bright light in the sky. It made them afraid, and they took it as a bad omen for Harold, and for England.

UNDER ATTACK

William of Normandy
Duke William was annoyed when he heard that Harold had been crowned king. He gathered together an army to invade and conquer England.

He persuaded Pope Alexander II to bless the expedition, and to send a special banner for his army. Knights and adventurers from many parts of Europe flocked to join William's force. But the core of the army was William's own Norman knights.

The Norwegians Invade
William was not the only person keen to conquer England. King Harald Hardrada of Norway also claimed the throne. He was supported by Harold II's outlawed brother, Tostig Godwinesson.

Harold was watching for William on the south coast when he heard of the Norwegian invasion. He marched north with an army of about 3,000 men.

Stamford Bridge

Harold and his army, now swollen by local troops, met the Norwegians at Stamford Bridge, near York.

There he met his traitor brother, and offered to restore his lands to him if he laid down his arms.

'What will you give my ally the King of Norway?' asked Tostig.

'Six feet of English ground,' said Harold. 'But as Hardrada is a giant, he shall have seven.'

In the battle which followed both Hardrada and Tostig were killed. But while Harold and his men were celebrating victory, news reached him that William had landed three days earlier.

The Normans Invade

William landed at Pevensey, in Sussex, and marched along the coast to Hastings, where he built a wooden castle.

Harold marched south to meet William, and reached London in five days. He waited there for five days to rest his weary men and for more troops to join him. Then he marched south to Hastings.

The two armies met at Sandlache, seven miles from Hastings (now the town of Battle). There were about 8,000 soldiers on each side.

THE INVADERS 47

1066 A.D.

The Battle of Hastings
The two leaders were the best generals of the day. William was cool and ruthless, while Harold was bold and impetuous. The Normans were better armed than the Saxons.

The battle lasted eight hours, much longer than most battles in those days. Harold and his brothers Gurth and Leofwin were killed. The leaderless Saxons retreated. They were unable to form another army, and the fate of England was decided.